HERMAN ®

VOLUME 4

CLASSICS

Published by ECW PRESS
2120 Queen Street East, Suite 200, Toronto, Ontario, Canada M4E 1E2

For HERMAN® permissions, licensing information,
and other product information, contact:
LaughingStock Licensing Inc.
P.O. Box 3006, Station C,
Ottawa, Ontario, Canada K1Y 4J3
(www.hermancomics.com)

HERMAN comics are distributed to newspapers worldwide by
United Media, 200 Madison Avenue, New York, NY, U.S.A. 10016

NATIONAL LIBRARY OF CANADA CATALOGUING IN PUBLICATION

Unger, Jim
Herman Classics / Jim Unger
ISBN 1-55022-616-9 (v. 1), ISBN 1-55022-657-6 (v. 2)
ISBN 1-55022-706-8 (v. 3), ISBN 1-55022-735-1 (v. 4)

I. Title.
NC1449.U48A4 2003   741.5'971   C2003-904330-4

DISTRIBUTION

CANADA: Jaguar Book Group, 100 Armstrong Avenue, Georgetown, Ontario, L7G 5S4

UNITED STATES: Independent Publishers Group, 814 North Franklin Street
Chicago, Illinois 60610

PRINTED AND BOUND IN CANADA

ECW PRESS
ecwpress.com

HERMAN®

— VOLUME 4 —

CLASSICS

by JIM Unger

ECW Press

"And now for a look at the latest picture from our weather satellite."

"Nice shot! That one crossed 12 lanes
and wiped out the coffee machine."

"I got the car in the garage, but I had
to drive it through the kitchen."

"Why do they call you, 'the elephant
man'? You look perfectly normal to me."

"I don't usually borrow stuff from
strangers, but I like your face."

"Did you hear *me* whining when your show was on?"

"Don't bother undressing. I'll turn up the power."

"Have you got any books on how to overcome shyness?"

"I'll get the check. Pass your money under the table."

"Biggest bug I ever saw!"

"I made two dozen chocolate chip cookies. Can you eat all of them?"

"D'you wanna stay here tonight or sleep on the beach and eat?"

"Anything for 22A?"

5

"When you grow up, make sure you marry a mechanic."

"My brother got a job in a wallpaper factory."

"One of you two will be my next sales manager."

"Your wife tells me you're making some bookshelves."

"The largest waist size we have
is 24 inches."

"Want me to try to get you
a private ward?"

"Cover your left eye, Madame."

"You've been overfeeding my horse
again, Smithers!"

"If you get any worse, can I keep your paint roller?"

"Can I buy one half and get the other half free?"

"Here, you want to be plant manager. Take care of this."

"I see you spent the last 12 years in the Navy."

"He needs a set by Friday."

"I know what you got me for my birthday. It was on the 11 o'clock news."

"As soon as I got married, I saved every spare nickel. Now I've got eight bucks."

"I told you yesterday — you can't come in without wearing a tie."

"Banana milkshake and two straws."

"Joycey, what's the best stuff
for split ends?"

"The invitation said 'informal dress'
so I borrowed one from my sister."

"Nobody's leaving! Why don't you start
singing one of your songs?"

"Eat this school report and let me do the talking."

"It's marked 'urgent' so I read it
on the way over."

"There's the bill and here's a photo
of my wife and kids."

"I need 400 of these and
a pair of hinges."

"Dad, I'm starting grade six soon.
I guess this is where the 'generation
gap' begins."

"You dropped your sheet
of glass back there!"

"He was an unmanageable 6' 2"
when I married him."

"Let's go, Rex. It's time for your
piano lessons."

"Room 1708 doesn't have a plug
for the bath!"

"Where are you hopping off to?"

"I'm looking for an uninhabited island with a fantastic night life."

"If we don't find a gas station soon, Wilkins, I'm going to have to take a rest."

"What was that cyclist shouting about back there?"

"They don't allow those on my planet."

"How did you say that without moving your lips?"

"Are these green ones emeralds?"

"Quick, put it on. Someone's coming!"

"Your honor, with 85 acquittals, my client has a faultless record."

"Your honor, before the jury retires to reach a verdict, my client wishes to present each of them with a little gift of jewelry."

"I'll have a coffee and a Danish to go."

"That guy who said the coffee tasted funny left without paying!"

"I don't mind you reading over my shoulder, but don't start doing the crossword puzzle."

"Are both of you suffering from double vision?"

"You're absolutely certain this one's mine?"

"If you're so smart, how come the world was in such a mess before I got here?"

"Tea! I said I wanted a small tea!"

"Haven't you got one in English?"

"He wants to give us $1,000 to use
the moon for a few days."

"Pull out as much as you want."

"Simpson, bring me an order of onion rings and move that candle further down the table."

"I fell asleep on the beach, reading the newspaper."

"Either you buy me a bike or I'm gonna get myself adopted."

"That was my ex-boyfriend's car!"

"If I get a good mark, you could be looking at a very nice apple tomorrow morning."

"I'll have a cheeseburger and
a root beer."

"I can't seem to make up my
mind about this one."

"Aw c'mon doc, let me
borrow a mirror."

"Welcome to planet Earth.
Is your mother home?"

"I'll take another bottle
of this after-shave."

"Here's one you'll love! Two weeks in an
open boat without food and water."

"The TV keeps switching back
to 'Wild Kingdom!'"

"I told you not to lay in the bath
all afternoon."

"All the cups are dirty. D'you want
your coffee in that?"

"Now I suppose you're gonna sulk
because I wouldn't give you
the afternoon off."

"As I wasn't too busy, I made you my
international award-winning
hamburger deluxe."

"Is the war over?"

HERMAN

JIM Unger

HOW INTERESTING...

SCIENTISTS BELIEVE THAT THERE ARE SOMETHING LIKE 400,000 BILLION SUNS IN OUR GALAXY ALONE...

IF ONLY 1 PERCENT HAD PLANETS AND ONLY 1 PERCENT OF THOSE COULD SUSTAIN LIFE...

THAT WOULD STILL LEAVE BILLIONS OF EARTHLIKE ENVIRONMENTS.

ISN'T THAT JUST MY LUCK.

I END UP ON THE SAME ONE AS YOU.

"Your friend Muriel is going through
Harry's pockets again!"

"Look, you're 103 years old, you've
got to start taking better care
of yourself."

"Have you got a 24-slice toaster?"

"The mailman's been here."

"Dad, a guy at school said we all came from humans."

"I was wondering how you'd play that shot."

"When are you going to face the fact that you're a lousy pickpocket?"

"You'd better remove your makeup. I've got some good news."

"Gimme 14 hot dogs."

"Will you keep the noise down? We're trying to have a party next door!"

"I don't mind the 17th floor as long as I have 64 sheets on my bed."

"Ignorance of the law is no excuse, buddy!"

"Can you change a $100 bill?"

"In your case, we have no interest at all."

"There's six billion of them down here!
Make sure none get on the ship
before we take off."

"As soon as he's finished, rush that
glass of water over to table nine."

"You're supposed to read it aloud!"

"Why did you move your plate?"

"According to the computer, we owe the gas company $14.3 billion for August."

"I like the color but won't the water keep running out?"

"A message from your grandson, sir."

"I asked him what he wanted for our anniversary and he said 'two minutes of silence.'"

"D'you mind if I take a photo? It's not often we get a 15-cent tip."

"So this is your wife, Dottie."

"The doctor thinks he's going to be very musical."

"I'll have to X-ray your arm again.
This one is overexposed."

"Oh, sweetheart! You're my
very first husband."

"George, how many years have I been
coming in this candy store?"

"I can't eat anymore of these
turquoise peas."

"This wildlife book you sold me is nothing but pictures of animals!"

"I hear you're looking for an aggressive salesman!"

"You're the one who kept telling me you were a 'go-getter.'"

"I don't really want a diagnosis. What diseases have you got for under $50?"

HERMAN

JIM Unger

COME IN, CRUDLEY.

CRUDLEY, THIS IS YOUR FOURTH YEAR AT THIS MEDICAL COLLEGE.

...AND I HAVE HERE YOUR HAND-WRITTEN EXAMINATION PAPERS.

NO ONE CAN UNDERSTAND A SINGLE WORD OF IT.

IT IS TOTALLY ILLEGIBLE.

WELL DONE.

"Look at that! Sixty-two-years-old
and not a single cavity."

"I'm your new secretary. Am I an hour
late or 23 hours early?"

"Is it too tight across the shoulders?"

"This is your loan application back
from our head office."

"It's a pity you're unemployed.
You need a couple of weeks off work."

"You don't look a day over 30 years old!"

"Here ... tell your mother we're out.
She won't believe me."

"I can't understand anyone
being afraid of dogs."

"You won't find a job in the
'Sports' section!"

"Cash or charge?"

"Remember, only bend the ones which
are not marked 'do not bend.'"

"You can sit there 'til I find out
where you hid my glasses!"

"It's homemade bread.
D'you want two slices?"

"Mother sent us each
a Christmas card."

"This rascal chased the wife's mother
20 feet up a tree."

"Two hamburgers, one coffee
and a bucket of water."

"I told you not to eat popcorn while you've got hiccups."

"Come on! Tell the nice man how much you want to borrow."

"Take one capsule tonight, and if there's no improvement by tomorrow morning, take the whole bottle."

"Fired already! You were only there five weeks."

"Up and left."

"They dropped the speeding charge but
I've got to pay for the three storefronts
and the railway station."

"I know it's your birthday soon,
but what can I buy a woman
who has everything?"

"I lost the key for my padlock!"

"Someone told me you'd had
a hair transplant."

"I wonder why they make these finger bandages so long?"

"I knew he was really sick. He hasn't complained about anything for three days."

"If I didn't love you I wouldn't eat your cooking, would I?"

"He's only been at his company for a year and already he's getting the minimum wage!"

"It's my new diet book."

"Be careful with the wine. I had trouble getting the cork out."

"Got a dog to fit that?"

"The peasants have stopped singing. Put the guard on 'red alert.'"

JIM *Unger*

YOU LOOK TIRED...

I'VE BEEN SITTING HERE ALL DAY THINKING HOW LUCKY I AM, HAVING A WIFE LIKE YOU.

NOT MANY WIVES WOULD GET A FULL-TIME FACTORY JOB TO HELP OUT WHEN THEIR HUSBAND GETS LAID OFF WORK...

...ESPECIALLY AT YOUR AGE.

DON'T THINK I DON'T APPRECIATE IT.

WHAT ARE WE HAVING FOR SUPPER?

"I'd ask you in, but I've only
got one chair."

"D'you buy used cats?"

"Whoever shouted 'Turkey' was correct."

"We can't stand here all day.
It must have jammed."

"Now scrape that off the carpet and serve it to him on a clean plate."

"I've found a secret room!"

"This is the last one he painted."

"Of course it's half eaten! You said you wanted the Chef's salad."

"I've never told anyone before, but
I was aiming at a crocodile."

"Was he as short as that in real life?"

"How am I supposed to know you're
allergic to these if you don't tell me!"

"We were wondering if we could
extend the maximum limit on
our charge account?"

"If you can spare the time, Williams, I'd like to see you in my office."

"You can't use your bookie as a reference."

"I'm having a fabulous evening, but I really must be home by 8 o'clock."

"Guy in the front row wants to know if you like blueberry or custard cream?"

"Can't you take a joke?"

"Coffee is 50 cents for the first half-hour and 30 cents for each additional half-hour."

"The top keeps flying off this food mixer."

"He seems to have decided on a baseball scholarship."

"Come on! Tell him you're sorry for stepping
on him at the top of the stairs."

"You wanna have good eyesight
if you go abroad, don't you?"

"Cindy's getting a job at a bank and
needs you as a reference."

"That robot that replaced you at work
has been laid off!"

"Let me know immediately if you start
feeling the urge to move sideways."

"Can you cut me a star-shaped piece
of glass to fit that hole?"

"We were finding it very hot
in here, Warden."

"She kept saying the dance
floor was lumpy."

"I think that dark shadow is where
I spilled some coffee."

"I would've been here sooner, but
our iceberg hit a ship."

"Nurse ... see if you can find
my little rubber hammer."

"Have you got any old bricks I can
take to my karate lesson?"

"Mrs. Baxter, I don't think things
are working out."

HERMAN

JIM Unger

I CAN'T READ THAT...

WHAT DOES IT SAY ON THE TELEVISION, I HAVEN'T GOT MY GLASSES...

IT SAYS, "WARNING. VIEWER DISCRETION ADVISED.....

"THE FOLLOWING GAME SHOW MAH NOT BE SUITABLE...

FOR ANYONE WITH AVERAGE...

OR ABOVE AVERAGE INTELLIGENCE."

"You're looking at the next general manager of 'Louie's Take-Out Pizza.'"

"Okay, you've got the job. On your mark, get set ..."

"Where did you put my book on archaeology?"

"Some of the guys at work are coming over this evening to help me do the laundry."

"He wasn't always bald. It's acid rain."

"My wife would like to look at some fur coats. Do you have a pair of binoculars?"

"And for the man who has everything, we have this personal nuclear deterrent."

"I think we've decided on the ruby-and-diamond cluster."

"This says you have a tendency
to grovel."

"I told you last week I had to work
late tonight!"

"We've been happily married for two
years — 1987 and 1989."

"I lost track of my age years ago.
I think I'm about 22."

"This is a much bigger apartment
than we're used to."

"I had over 200 hours of flying time
when I was your age."

"Did you or did you not tell him
I was a Homo sapiens?"

"I sold half the business."

"You'd be surprised how many people walk out without paying!"

"In 35 years, you're my first case of this!"

"We're out of vitamins."

"Forgot the cat's birthday, didn't you?"

"Is that the man who tried to mug you?"

"You were going to fix the screen door
six months ago!"

"Make sure he pays cash."

"We had much nicer diseases
when I was a girl."

"The only time he's got a 48-inch chest
is when he stands on his head!"

"Nurse, you'd better put these on."

"Separate checks, please."

"I think my memory's coming back!
Ask me who won the World Series
in 1200 B.C."

"Make sure he's home in an hour."

"Wanna go see a movie, baby?"

"Of course, we're looking for a man who can work without supervision."

"She's here to get some entry forms for the Miss Universe competition."

"I can't explain now but I have been called away on business for three months."

65

"It works most of the time."

"OK, don't start showing off!"

"When was this passport photo taken?"

"I've lost the key."

"Ralph, what's the price on
these lizard's feet?"

"Can you see anything?"

"He shot it in the desert."

"Your honor, my client thinks ten
years is a little harsh and requests
permission to approach the bench."

"Got a room with a panoramic
view of the city?"

"I won't be home Friday. They've
changed all the locks."

"I'll skip the dessert menu. I don't like
too many surprises in one day."

"Just relax and get your memory back.
Don't lay there worrying about the fifty
bucks you owe me."

"I knew we shouldn't have bought
waterfront property."

"I ordered a coffee when I came in. When
will the beans leave South America?"

"I finally found his credit cards, taped
inside the TV cabinet."

"Do you have such a thing as
a refrigerator with a revolving door?"

"Of the smaller breeds, these are
about the best guard dogs."

"We had to remove your brain for
a couple of days, so just try to relax."

"If we have to go in there again
it will save you a bundle."

"Open up! I want to take a look
down your throat."

"I could literally double my income
with a 20-foot ladder."

"I've got a stabbing pain
in my left kidney."

"I want you to take one of these
with water every four years."

"I guess I'll plead not guilty just
to get the old ball rolling."

"I want you to walk two miles a day ...
and take my dog with you."

"I thought I made it clear that they had to be back in their bowl by eight o'clock!"

"I see the dollar's taken another beating."

"I hope you had a radio transmitter on that ball!"

"Are you the guy who advertised he'd found a wallet?"

"Whoever heard of anyone studying
for an eye examination?"

"I told you it was supposed to go
around your neck."

"Stand away from that on/off switch."

"If you want a picture, you gotta
keep your head still!"

JUST KEEP QUIET.

YOU TOLD THE IMMIGRATION OFFICE AT THE AIRPORT THAT YOU WERE FROM CUBA AND YOU WANTED TO DEFECT.

BUT NOW WE FIND YOU'RE AN INSURANCE AGENT FROM CLEVELAND RETURNING FROM A WEEK'S VACATION IN MEXICO.

WHAT I WANT TO KNOW IS ...

WHY?

HE HATES LINE-UPS.

75

"Hey, Lily! Was it 1958 I got my bronze medal for the 'foxtrot?'"

"I just seem to be walking around in circles all day!"

"Can't you help me catch the canary?"

"Anything under $25,000 nowadays is considered 'junk jewelry.'"

"My daughter tells me you're hoping
for a career in shipping."

"Here, take this, but make sure you
get home in 90 seconds."

"Put your stupid hands down; he's
looking for the dentist."

"Old George has been with the company
38 years. Do I hear $300?"

"Is this the guy who was stuck in the elevator for three days?"

"He jumped a motorcycle across the Grand Canyon!"

"He wants to sit with his back to the wall."

"We need a six-foot ladder and an eight-foot ladder."

"Lily, run upstairs and see if this guy's
gas barbecue is in our bedroom."

"It's got a two-level finished basement."

"Table for three."

"As we'll be flying over water,
I'll demonstrate what to do in the
case of a shark attack."

"I take it your business meeting
was a success."

"Don't keep saying 'I do.'
You're the best man."

"I know it's probably uncomfortable,
but we need them as evidence."

"I'm campaigning for the little guy."

"You're not allowed to take it out yourself."

"Wilson, don't drag your fingernails
down the blackboard."

"I'm sorry, sir, that's not
hand luggage."

"You need plenty of rest. You'd better
stay in the gutter for a few days."

"Your teeth are fantastic, but your
gums have to come out."

"Take off your tie and unbutton your shirt. There are nine women on the jury."

"This is Dr. Elgin, our expert on tropical diseases."

"Here we go! Step one: Take off your shirt."

"Your brother-in-law is marooned on a desert island."

"I'm sure he couldn't have done
it intentionally!"

"You were stronger on our
first honeymoon."

"Any questions so far?"

"My report card isn't bad if you consider
the genes I have to work with."

"Your boss didn't want you to lie here
worrying about the work piling up,
so he fired you."

"Breathe deeply and take a quick
look at my bill."

"I don't know who he is! He was there
when I woke up this morning."

"Can I go in first?"

"Did you tell the cat he could
have my striped shirt?"

"This is new ... 'mega-puncture.'"

"Got any nice gift-wrapping paper?"

"He wants another 50 bucks ... full house, jacks and nines."

"You've got the job. Now, take these home and practice kissing them."

"Quick, drink this! It'll settle your stomach."

"You're a little underweight. Put this in your pocket."

"Mr. White is here for his annual checkup, doctor."

"She gave me a box of chocolates for my birthday with all the soft centers missing."

"It's not catching, is it?"

"I'm sorry! He's taking karate lessons."

"Did you say on the phone you were 'in your 20s' or 'born in the '20s?'"

"I'm sorry. I haven't laughed like this for months."

"I need to borrow your 68 cents of 'mad money.'"

"Is it okay if Vanessa chooses one for herself?"

"I think my test results are a pretty good indication of your abilities as a teacher."

"I married her for looks and she married
me for money. Now we're even."

"Your honor, a 25-year jail sentence
would jeopardize my client's job
at the supermarket."

"This should hold it!"

"It says, 'Your day will be greatly
influenced by the planet Neptune.'"

"I'm sorry, sir, visiting hours are over."

"These are for you in court. We're going for 'insanity.'"

"Don't let George scare you. He's in for art forgery."

"Here's the menu. I'll be back in a couple of hours."

"One minute, 52 seconds. I could
have died of thirst!"

"Dad, I'm writing my life story.
Is 'poverty-stricken' one word?"

"Is it still half price for kids?"

"For $12, I'll have to keep them
in our safety deposit box."

HERMAN

JIM Unger

SILENCE IN COURT.

I HAVE REVIEWED ALL THE EVIDENCE IN THIS CASE...

CONSIDERING YOU HAVE BEEN MARRIED FOR 12 YEARS...

I'M GOING TO SEE THAT YOUR EX-WIFE GETS $250 PER WEEK.

WE BOTH APPRECIATE THAT, YOUR HONOR.

... I'LL SEND AN EXTRA 50 BUCKS FROM ME.

"I used to have a bigger eye chart,
but I wasn't making any money."

"Can we borrow your coat? We're
going to the movies."

"Marriage is a partnership. I eat your
cooking so you wash the dishes."

"Old Rex has been in the family for
as far back as I can remember."

"We already ate at home. We just want to see how much we saved."

"Nothing on?"

"I gave up two hours of sleep to apply for this job!"

"D'you have any other references apart from this one from your mother?"

"Get a move on. The tranquilizer
dart's wearing off."

"I think I'm gonna get the job.
Call me back in five minutes."

"We need something fast for
about 10 minutes."

"Just cut off a dollar's worth."

"D'you still want the 'catch of the day?'"

"What's so dumb about cutting out
a full-page advertisement?"

"My stomach's having a tough time
getting used to good food."

"We're on our second honeymoon.
Make sure our rooms are not
too close together."

"He's probably taking a breather
on his way north."

"People are beginning to complain about
too much violence on cave walls."

"The guy at the pet store said
he needs more exercise."

"You can earn $504 a week if you
work the full 168 hours."

"I'm sure you've all been anxious to meet
our new company chairman."

"This guy wants to borrow our ladder."

"If you insist on laughing, sir, I must ask you to browse in the humor section."

"He's back!"

"Stay away from those wooden ones. I nearly got my head blown off!"

"This is not an illegal strike.
We're having a 72-hour lunch break."

"Come on, Herbert, look lively.
The gates open in five minutes."

"It's not my fault if my dad
won't lend me the car!"

"I'll have to deduct five points
for cornering on two wheels."

"We got a nice postcard from those
little green guys in the U.F.O."

"He still won't talk."

"D'you know how many people are hit
by lightning every year?"

"I had to make a videotape of myself
telling him his supper's ready."

HERMAN

JIM Unger

WOULDN'T IT BE GREAT...

IMAGINE IF THERE WAS A COUNTRY WHERE EVERYONE HAD TO BE FRIENDLY AND COURTEOUS ALL THE TIME...

WHERE NO ONE BROKE THE LAW AND EVERYONE DROVE WITHIN THE SPEED LIMITS...

THERE'S ONLY ONE THING WRONG WITH THAT.

WHAT'S THAT?

THEY WOULDN'T LET YOU LIVE THERE.

"OK, you've got the job. But you make sure you have a big breakfast before coming to work."

"You'd better hurry up and decide. The warranty runs out in 15 minutes."

"Come on. You were all excited when you saw it on TV."

"C'mon, Dave! I saw him first."

"I've seen it before. He's changing
into a butterfly."

"What do you mean, you don't
recognize this court?"

"I'm-fine-how-are-you?"

"You haven't eaten your chicken!"

"I wish you would put your razor away."

"I'm gonna let you go this time,
but stick to the speed limit."

"This isn't the correct water pump,
but I'll make it fit."

"Keep your head down, Billy-Joe."

"I'm putting you down as 'potential donor material.'"

"Something just landed on my back!"

"Got any more of those blue-and-white striped ones that taste like tuna?"

"Let go, sweetheart, and Mommy will give you this bone."

"I suppose you heard about that blonde who used to work at the bank ..."

"I gotta open you up again. Those things are $36 a pair!"

"Can you stand on your right leg?"

"If he had six wives, how come there was no Henry the Ninth?"

"You gotta be real fast when you're painting ducks."

"Did you have your hair done at that new place on Market Street?"

"Give me your credit card. I'm getting these for your birthday."

"I'm sorry, Wilson. After 16 years of loyal service, you're being replaced by this microchip."

"I just hope that's not the water you had your teeth in!"

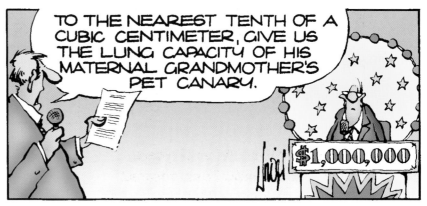

115

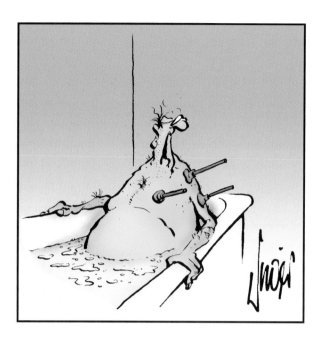

"What time do those kids go to bed?"

"We've decided on a small wedding.
I'm not going."

"She said if I don't finish painting this
fence in time, I won't be able to go to
her sister's wedding this afternoon."

"Rub this on your feet three times
a day, during meals."

"Fish and chips for one and
28 chef salads."

"You should stay off that left foot
for a couple of days."

"Don't play with Grampa's foot."

"The doctor said you can come home
on Friday if I get rid of the cat."

"Get a move on! She'll be home in 10 minutes."

"How d'you expect people to read labels that are upside down?"

"According to this, we gave a 45-year-old woman a skin rash."

"Is your wife still taking
singing lessons?"

"Dear Pinkie: Having a wonderful
time in the south of France."

"Listen, Ron, I'm not going
bowling tonight."

"It never ceases to amaze me
what people throw away."

"Table for two ... name of 'Kong.'"

"He's out! Can I take a message?"

"Lily, see if there's anything on the
six o'clock news about it."

"Large coffee to go and make sure
the lid's on tight."

"Some florist delivered a bunch
of flowers here by mistake."

"I brought him over because I want
him to apologize."

"Forty words per minute doesn't
include spelling."

"No, sir. This is not a Greek restaurant.
You have the menu upside down."

"I can't help you if you're just going to sit there mooing."

"We usually put 30 percent on!"

"The doctor says he has to have plenty of rest for the next few days."

"You're getting overheated. Go outside in the fresh air and clean the windows."

"Your birthday gift is in the garage, charging up the car battery."

"Is it true you like your employees to speak their minds, Big Nose?"

"Which parent do you want to sign it: my mother, my stepfather, my mother's third husband, or my natural father's fourth wife who lives with us?"

"Not him?!"

"My goodness! It says in another
month, I'll be charging $20 a visit."

"George, have we got 900 rolls
of this 'imitation stone?'"

"Think back ... two years ago ...
you sold me a gerbil."

"What are you doing now?
Throw the Frisbee."

"You say you spent five years
at the North Pole?"

"You'll be pleased to know, madame, we
just landed safely at the airport."

"Cost me $60 and she only
wore it twice."

"Don't look like that. You'll be boasting
about this for the rest of your life."

"When are you gonna start
facing reality?"

"I've worn a 34-inch waist ever
since I was a teenager."

"Er ... stay cool, baby ... and, er
... what's happening?"

"Will you quit whimpering?
I'm cleaning my glasses!"

"It's been six days. Has he reported
me missing yet?"

"D for Destiny's Child, E for Eminem,
A for Alanis, and R for Rolling Stones."

"You're an hour late! Don't blame me if
your cheese sandwich is ruined."

"The changing room is occupied. Crouch
down behind the tie rack."

"I'll have your red snapper, white
potatoes and green beans. D'you
have any orange carrots?"

"I spoke to the doctor. He said you're taking too much iron."

"A spot of car trouble, officer. My chauffeur's gone for a tow truck."

"I'd like to see a set of your unbreakable dishes."

"He really likes you!"

"Well, I sure wasn't making any money as a pet store."

"I got her in a poker game. I had a pair of eights and the other guy had three jacks."

"I hear your husband is a ventriloquist."

"Take up the slack."

HERMAN

JIM Unger

YOUR BREAKFAST IS GETTING COLD.

DID YOU SEE THIS! A WOMAN WAS GRANTED A DIVORCE BECAUSE HER HUSBAND VERBALLY ABUSED HER IN THE PET FOOD SECTION OF A SUPERMARKET.

...SHE GETS TO KEEP THE HOUSE...

...THE CAR...

...ALL THE FURNITURE.

...AND CUSTODY OF THE NINETY-EIGHT CATS.

"I'm planning a solo voyage around
the world. D'you want to
come with me?"

"Now, let's see. You say yours has
three little blue dots on it?"

"I don't normally buy bug spray at
the door, but the one we're using
obviously doesn't work."

"I see you finally fixed the crack
in the wall."

"I hear you're giving a series of lectures on bodybuilding."

"You've broken my best flowerpot!"

"Well, you knew we had only one tree when you bought it."

"That's the last pair I have in those!"

"Just out of idle curiosity, how d'you manage to serve leftovers 14 days in a row?"

"You're not staying home from work. It's payday."

"Dougie, have we got these in coral pink?"

"And just where have you been at three o'clock in the morning?"

"She wants six chicken wings.
Three left and three right."

"Take two before you go to bed and
before you wake up."

"Is that what they teach you
at mailman's college?"

"Whaddya mean you don't know what
it is? Who cooked it?"

"Port?! Starboard?! Can't you speak English?"

"Hello, Frank. Does my insurance cover me for snapped-off needles?"

"I'm starting my vacation tomorrow, so I'll leave you 14 newspapers."

"Obviously you weren't at the meeting this morning."

"OK, that's enough for one day.
I'll see you next Tuesday."

"When I was your age, I could do the 100-yard dash in 12 minutes!"

"What do you mean, my blood pressure pills aren't working?!"

"Do you have any other hobbies besides 'bird watching?'"

"The computer handles all our loan applications."

"One egg sandwich with live entertainment, $12.50."

"Mention something about her not fooling around with my stereo equipment."

"Same old Christmas. He bought me a power saw and I bought him gold earrings."

"Today's special is spaghetti and meatballs."

"Dad took us to Sea World and fell in."

"Solid as a rock and light
as a feather."

"Will you get a move on with those
loafers? He's trying to leave!"

HERMAN

JIM Unger

SIX MINUTES.

OK .... YOU HAVE FIVE MORE MINUTES TO FINISH DRAWING A MAP OF THE WORLD.

I'M GONNA NEED MORE TIME AND MORE PAPER.

HOW FAR HAVE YOU GOTTEN?

I'M UP TO THE FISH SHOP ON THE HIGH STREET.

"He keeps forgetting his name!"

"I explained the risks to his wife
and she thinks we should
take a chance."

"We're closing in five minutes.
I'll get you a blanket."

"I got 14 days without parole! Don't
waste your life. Find someone else."

"I need one more gallon of
that ceiling white."

"It's a little round white thing;
comes out of a chicken."

"They took away all my mink coats and
my diamond-encrusted wristwatch."

"Somebody tell that new assistant
manager I found his sport jacket."

"My cousin Herbie's at
a zoo in America."

"Did anyone other than yourself
know the combination?"

"Is there such a thing as a bathroom
scale fitted with shock absorbers?"

"I haven't seen one of these for years."

"And don't let me find out you're
having a good time."

"I think we can dispense with hand
signals in the middle of
the Pacific Ocean."

"I didn't bring my glasses. Does that
say you've been pardoned?"

"Here's the latest word on that mystery
object seen over our city this evening."

"I've come to ask for your daughter's hand in moving my furniture."

"Can't you see I'm eating? Why don't you push off and go look at the penguins?"

"What's it gonna be: Go for walkies, or have this bone and watch the game on TV?"

"What about monkeys? You must have monkeys!"

"It says right here. You're not supposed to open the lid during the spin cycle."

"What really bugs me is I can't
remember what I did."

"Mrs. Rodriguez, next Monday I want
you to stand in for me at the annual
stockholders meeting."

"Randolph! Your blind date is here."

"See if you can get a saber-toothed
tiger for the weekend. And make
sure it's not all fat."

"I called your receptionist this morning for a 3 o'clock appointment to have my eyes tested."

"I told you you'd love it."

"I've only got a few minutes. Where are the short stories?"

"These will stop you tossing and turning all night."

"We're living in very strange times, Martha."

"Clamp!"

"I'm making you Dobson's personal assistant until his feet get better."

"Who said 'No man is an island?'"

"I think this one is yours."

"Your four years' hard work
in the basement just came waltzing
up the stairs."

"I think you'll enjoy working here.
We're very informal."

"They all want coffee."

"It was a choice between one of these
or a dozen skimpy little roses."

"Dropping out of school never
done me no harm."

"I wish I could lay around in bed all day
every time I had a sore throat."

"Don't touch that volume control."

"What's the matter with you?
That's the third time you've knocked
over the coffee."

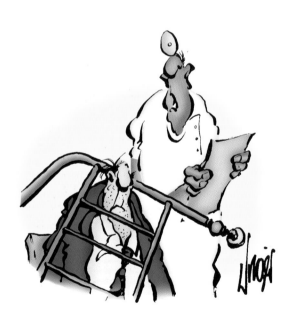

"You still having trouble sleeping?"

"Imagine them wanting a $5
delivery charge!"

"Have you got one with
an eye-level grill?"

"OK. Here he comes. Now remember
everything I taught you."

"Miss Stokes, I've been looking at
your work record, and you're taking
far too many days off."

"I'm back!"

"He's down in the basement
cleaning the furnace."

"Anybody wanna cross the street?"

"My daughter tells me you're
a lifeguard."

"I nearly didn't come with all that rain."

"I don't want that right
in front of the TV."

"You'd be in a lousy mood, too,
if you had to deal with twits
like this every day."

"I'm not nagging. I just said I hope
you're not going to ruin my
sister's wedding."

"I used to have a dog, but he wouldn't
eat my wife's leftovers."

"Here's a nice two-bedroom apartment, but they don't allow pets."

"If you don't mind me saying so, sir, he never did take well to captivity."

"Arnold, where can I lay my hands on a fan belt for a 2078 Cosmos Star cruiser?"

"Of course I remembered your birthday! I had a drink with the guys at lunchtime."

"We had a trial separation,
but she found me."

"... and cancel the tickets to Acapulco."

"Did I tell you I was voted 'The boy
most likely to go somewhere?'"

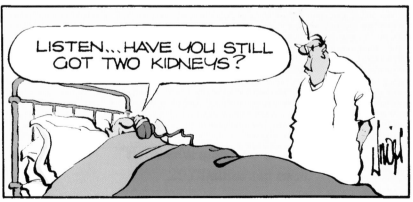

"I'll be honest with you, this is not the largest planet in the universe."

"Why would I take your pipe? Have you looked in the kitchen?"

"Is that 'turkey with noodles,' 'beef with cabbage' or 'lasagna?'"

"I thought your résumé said you did 40 words a minute."

"Let's see. ... Your wife had a baby girl at 2:15 a.m., a boy at 2:20 a.m. and another two girls at 2:25 a.m."

"When we get home, pretend you're out of breath."

"If it looks like a close finish, jump off."

"Bill specializes in the study of rare diseases."

"I've still got a few wrinkles
to iron out."

"You wouldn't believe the time we had
getting him down those stairs."

"Your previous employer says
you're unpredictable."

"This will take about 20 minutes."

"Anyone here eat the pork chops?"

"Someone's been taking shots
at the decoy!"

"It's me. I think I'm having a nightmare.
Check and see if I'm in bed."

"He's a bit nervous."

"What do you want on
your hamburger?"

"Nice job, Percy. See you next time."

"The wife used to do quite a bit
of modeling ... until she lost
her tube of glue."

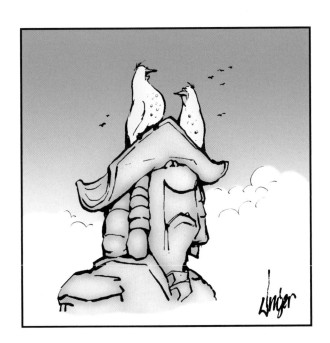

"I think these older statues are
a lot more comfortable than
modern sculpture."

"She hid all my clothes so I couldn't
go out tonight."

"The housewarming party has been postponed."

"If you want to be a grandfather, you've got to make a few sacrifices."

"He was only 35 years old when he did that one."

"OK. You can put your clothes back on."

175

"So I said, 'If you wanted to do something useful around here, why don't you paint the fence?'"

"Thank you, Burrows, for that descriptive insight into polluting the environment."

"Very impressive credentials. How do you feel about relocating to another planet?"

"How was I supposed to know it fired torpedoes?"

"Does that say, 'Learn to read in seven days?'"

"I feel a lot better since I ran out of those pills you gave me."

"Have you got another menu? I can't afford anything on this one."

"Do you have any special plans
for this pork chop?"

"When he said he wanted to speak to
'the man with the forked tongue,' I
assumed he meant a lawyer."

"Good grief, man. It's only
a parking ticket!"

"Detective Parker, zoo patrol."

"You'd better cancel the rest of my appointments."

"Run out back and stick 'Happy Birthday' on that for me."

"He'll be 42 years old next month."

"I'm sorry, sir, I just can't find yours anywhere."

"Cheese omelet, sunny side up."

"Catch of the day is the egg salad sandwich for $6."

"Your mother's been at my wine again."

"OK, five more minutes, then we'll go somewhere else."

"I hate bothering you, but my wife wants to know if she passed her driver's test."

"So much for your theory that
the Earth is round."

"Mildew, I'm not accusing you, but
there's a grape missing."

"Chest, 68."

"Personally, I think it's all these
chemicals they spray on the fruit."

"I need some books about this wide."

"That's the last time we'll
use this hospital!"

"These are normally $1,000 shirts."

"Your job application says you
like meeting the public."

"I'll have a cheeseburger with everything on it except cheese."

"Whaddya mean, 'The strawberries aren't fresh?' I just opened the can five minutes ago!"

"I need a dishwasher that can handle heavy baked-on grease — three times a day."

"I just got a late score. Romans 2,168; Carthaginians 1,804."

"That's $194.32, less four cents for the bonus coupon."

"Here, work your way through that lot and I'll go easy on you next year."

"These all suddenly disappeared about 2 million years ago."

"What did you expect to find in oxtail soup?"

"Two bedrooms."

"Did Grandpa give you permission
to take that off his bad leg?"

"Fourteen shopping minutes
to Christmas!"

"Just give him your money, dear.
The last one sued us for
his medical bills."

"How do you spell 'escapologist?'"

"Gimme a stale donut and cold coffee."